ACKNOWLEDGMENT

Resurgence Books would like to acknowledge the talent of Chrissie Wright in the crafting of these children's materials. This series would not have been possible without her expertise in children's education and her discerning mind for sound, engaging, and age-appropriate theology.

Thank you, Chrissie.

Lost and Found Kids: 7+ Workbook
Teaching God's Story from Creation to Kingdom Come

Published by Resurgence Publishing 1411 NW 50th Street

Seattle, WA 98107

First printing, 2012 Printed in the United States of America

ISBN-13: 978-1-938805-09-7

TABLE OF CONTENTS

STEWARDSHIP

KINGDOM

WHAT'S IN THIS BOOK?

This is the workbook kids ages seven and up will use every week as you learn about new doctrines, and how they connect to God's Big Story with Jesus as Hero. Read on to find out what you will be doing each week to help you learn about who God is and who you are.

FOCUS ACTIVITY

This is what you will do when you enter your classroom. The Focus Activity will help get you ready for the day's lesson: it will either get you thinking about what you already know, or connect the day's Big Idea to some experiences in your own life.

ACTIVITY

This is what you will complete in your Community Group to help what you learned in the lesson stick in your brain.

SCRIPTURE EXPLORATION

This page will help you understand the Bible verse you are studying. You will spend two weeks on each verse.

TRINITY: Lesson 1, Focus Activity

In just two sentences, write as much as you can about what you know about the Trinity.

Now, write a list of three-word phrases that describe what you know about God.

Example:	*God*	*is*	*powerful*

TRINITY: Lesson 1, Activity

Write the verse below.	*Which persons of the Trinity are mentioned here?*	*What does this verse say to me about the character of God?*
Genesis 1:26a		
Matthew 28:19		
Titus 3:4–6		

TRINITY: Lesson 1, Scripture Exploration

"And when Jesus was baptized, immediately he went up from the water, and behold, the heavens were opened to him, and he saw the Spirit of God descending like a dove and coming to rest on him; and behold, a voice from heaven said, 'This is my beloved Son, with whom I am well pleased.'"

—Matthew 3:16–17

1. Circle all the words that refer to God the Father.
2. Put a box around all the words that refer to Jesus the Son.
3. Underline all the words that refer to the Holy Spirit.
4. In your own words, what is going on in this verse?

TRINITY: Lesson 2, Focus Activity

In the spaces below, write a two-sentence summary describing what you know about each person of the Trinity.

God the Father

God the Son (Jesus)

God the Holy Spirit

TRINITY: Lesson 2, Activity

Person of the Trinity	*In my own words, this person's special job is to . . .*
GOD THE FATHER	
GOD THE SON (JESUS)	
GOD THE HOLY SPIRIT	

TRINITY: Lesson 2, Scripture Exploration

Review the verses you started to explore last week.

"And when Jesus was baptized, immediately he went up from the water, and behold, the heavens were opened to him, and he saw the Spirit of God descending like a dove and coming to rest on him; and behold, a voice from heaven said, 'This is my beloved Son, with whom I am well pleased.'"

—Matthew 3:16–17

1. Circle all the words that refer to God the Father.
2. Put a box around all the words that refer to Jesus the Son.
3. Underline all the words that refer to the Holy Spirit.
4. How does this verse connect to your own life?

TRINITY: Lesson 3, Focus Activity

What do you know about the Trinity?
Fill in the letters of the acrostic below with phrases or sentences that tell about the Trinity. (The first line has been completed as an example.)

T here is only one God.

R

I

N

I

T

Y

TRINITY: Lesson 3, Activity

Write the verse below.	*Which persons of the Trinity are mentioned here?*	*What does this verse say to me about God as Friend?*
John 5:20		
John 14:31		
Matthew 6:10		

TRINITY: Lesson 3, Scripture Exploration

"The Father loves the Son and has given all things into his hand."

—John 3:35

1. Circle any words that refer to God the Father.
2. Put a box around any words that refer to God the Son.
3. Underline any action words (verbs) that describe what the Father does for the Son as Friend.
4. What does this verse say to you about the kind of Friend God is?

TRINITY: Lesson 4, Focus Activity

God is a Friend, and God has Friends. Fill in the letters of the acrostic below with phrases or sentences that tell about the three persons of the Trinity as Friends. (The first line has been completed as an example.)

Forever friends

R

I

E

N

D

S

TRINITY: Lesson 4, Activity

In just two minutes, write some thoughts in response to the following question:

HOW DOES KNOWING GOD THE TRINITY CHANGE THE WAY WE LIVE?

TRINITY: Lesson 4, Scripture Exploration

Review the verse you started to explore last week.

"The Father loves the Son and has given all things into his hand."

—John 3:35

1. Circle any words that refer to God the Father.
2. Put a box around any words that refer to God the Son.
3. Underline any action words (verbs) that describe what the Father does for the Son as Friend.
4. How does this verse connect to your own life?

REVELATION: Lesson 1, Focus Activity

Imagine that you are a screenwriter. Write one page from a movie script describing the most beautiful place in the world you can think of. Include details of at least three things that you would see there, using as many descriptive words as possible.

REVELATION: Lesson 1, Activity

Jesus is a Rescuer. When he changes your heart and adopts you as son or daughter, he keeps on loving you and loving you even when you fail. Your sin makes him sad, but he fully paid for it on the cross and he chooses to forgive you and love you over and over. Then, the more you realize who Jesus is, the more you want to obey him! You obey because he loves you, not to make him love you.

Let's take a look at a man from the Bible and how Jesus responded to him.

1. Read Luke 22:31–34 and 54–61.

   In your own words, what is going on here?

2. Now, read Luke 24:36–44.

   In your own words, what is going on here? How does Jesus respond to Peter?

How does Jesus respond to you? Can you find any passages in the Bible where God speaks to you about how he is a Friend to you in the face of your sin?

REVELATION: Lesson 1, Scripture Exploration

"The heavens declare the glory of God, and the sky above proclaims his handiwork."

—Psalm 19:1

1. Circle any words that refer to things that God the Trinity has made.
2. Put a box around any words that refer to God.
3. Underline any words that mean the same thing as "said."
4. In your own words, what is this verse saying? What do the heavens and the sky show you?

REVELATION: Lesson 2, Focus Activity

Write a one-page movie script about a time when you knew the right thing to do. Include yourself and at least one other character.

Now stop and consider . . .

Who created your conscience?

REVELATION: Lesson 2, Activity

In the frame below, draw a speed sketch of a time when your conscience told you that something was wrong. (Add words if you'd like!)

Consider some more . . .

How did you know it was wrong? Where did your sense of wrong come from?

REVELATION: Lesson 2, Scripture Exploration

Review the verse you started to explore last week.

"The heavens declare the glory of God, and the sky above proclaims his handiwork."

—Psalm 19:1

1. Circle any words that refer to things that God the Trinity has made.
2. Put a box around any words that refer to God.
3. Underline any words that mean the same thing as "said."
4. How does this verse connect to your own life?

REVELATION: Lesson 3, Focus Activity

Write a list of three-word phrases that describe places or ways you learn about God.

Example:	*From*	*my*	*dad*

Circle above the place or way that you learn about God the most often, and draw a speed sketch of it in the frame below.

REVELATION: Lesson 3, Activity

In your own words, answer: Does God want just some people to know about himself? Why?

REVELATION: Lesson 3, Scripture Exploration

"All Scripture is breathed out by God and profitable for teaching, for reproof, for correction, and for training in righteousness."

—2 Timothy 3:16

1. Underline the words you know.
2. In your own words, answer: What do the words you already know tell you about the Bible?

3. Circle the words that seem tricky.
4. Write the words that seem tricky to you in the table below, then use a tool to help you figure out what each word might mean.

Tricky Word	What might it mean? (Use tools like your friends in Community Group, your Community Group leader, your Bible, or a dictionary.)

REVELATION: Lesson 4, Focus Activity

Write a list of three-word phrases that describe what you know about the Bible. Try to remember some of the details you learned about Scripture last week.

Example: *Comes* *from* *God*

REVELATION: Lesson 4, Activity

Read the following verses from Genesis—these are God's words that he planned for us to hear! When you finish reading, follow the directions at the bottom of the page.

"And God said, 'Let there be light,' and there was light."

—Genesis 1:3

"And God said, 'Let there be an expanse in the midst of the waters, and let it separate the waters from the waters.'"

—Genesis 1:6

"And God said, 'Let the waters under the heavens be gathered together into one place, and let the dry land appear.' And it was so."

—Genesis 1:9

"And God said, 'Let the earth sprout vegetation, plants yielding seed, and fruit trees bearing fruit in which is their seed, each according to its kind, on the earth.' And it was so."

—Genesis 1:11

"And God said, 'Let the earth bring forth living creatures according to their kinds—livestock and creeping things and beasts of the earth according to their kinds.' And it was so."

—Genesis 1:24

"Then God said, 'Let us make man in our image, after our likeness. And let them have dominion over the fish of the sea and over the birds of the heavens and over the livestock and over all the earth and over every creeping thing that creeps on the earth."

—Genesis 1:26

Now go back and circle the third word in each verse.

REVELATION: Lesson 4, Scripture Exploration

Review the verse you started to explore last week.

"All Scripture is breathed out by God and profitable for teaching, for reproof, for correction, and for training in righteousness."

—2 Timothy 3:16

1. Underline the words you know.
2. In your own words, answer: What do the words you already know tell you about the Bible?

3. Circle the words that seem tricky.
4. How does this verse connect to your own life?

CREATION: Lesson 1, Focus Activity

To get yourself thinking, write a speed summary of everything you already know about how God created the world.

If you have time, sketch a quick picture of what you think the world looked like after God's seven days of creation.

CREATION: Lesson 1, Activity

What are some things God created that you really love? Sketch the first three things that come to mind in the boxes below.

CREATION: Lesson 1, Scripture Exploration

Write the verse below.	*In your own words, what is this verse saying?*	*How does this verse add to what you already know about creation?*
Genesis 1:1		
Job 12:10		

CREATION: Lesson 2, Focus Activity

Who takes care of you at home?

Who or what do you take care of?

Brainstorm examples of each in the lists below.

.... takes care of me by:

- ....
- ....
- ....
- ....
- ....

I take care of .... by:

- ....
- ....
- ....
- ....
- ....

CREATION: Lesson 2, Activity

God launched his Rescue Plan by creating the world out of nothing. Jesus lived, died, and rose to live out the Rescue Plan, and God keeps on taking care of the world while his Story continues. He even lets us be part of his Big Story by paying for our sin and changing our hearts to love him and know we need his forgiveness.

Let's stop and think about God's Big Story. Sketch and label a timeline with snapshots from God's Big Story.

The start of the Story:	*The Rescue Scene:*	*The scene you're living in:*	*How the Story ends:*

CREATION: Lesson 2, Scripture Exploration

Write the verse below.	*In your own words, what is this verse saying?*	*How does this verse add to what you already know about creation?*
Acts 17:28		
Colossians 1:15–17		

CREATION: Lesson 3, Focus Activity

Write a list of three-word phrases that describe gifts that God has given you for his glory. These are all things you can thank God for!

I can thank God for . . .

Example:	*Really*	*orange*	*sunsets*

Circle one of the gifts you wrote on your list and draw a speed sketch of it in the frame below. Feel free to add words thanking God for his gift.

CREATION: Lesson 3, Activity

Think of a time when you thanked God for something. What was it? How were you feeling? What did you say to God? Were you worshiping him? (If you're having trouble, can you think of a time you heard someone else thanking God? What did you notice?)

CREATION: Lesson 3, Scripture Exploration

"And one called to another and said: 'Holy, holy, holy is the LORD of hosts; the whole earth is full of his glory!'"

—Isaiah 6:3

1. Who is speaking in this verse? (Read Isaiah 6:1–2 for clues.)

2. Who is the speaker talking about? Circle the name in the verse.
3. What is the speaker doing in this verse? Why are they talking?

4. What is filled with God's glory? Circle the words.

CREATION: Lesson 4, Focus Activity

Think of a time when you have said "Thank you" for something. It could be for a gift someone gave you, or for something that someone did for you. On the lines below, tell the story of what you were grateful for.

CREATION: Lesson 4, Activity

Circle the word GLORY in the verse.	*OT or NT?*	*Identify the WHO and/or WHAT in this verse. WHO gets glory? WHAT brings him glory?*	*HOW does this connect to your own life?*
Psalm 96:3: "Declare his glory among the nations, his marvelous works among all the peoples!"			
Psalm 115:1: "Not to us, O LORD, not to us, but to your name give glory, for the sake of your steadfast love and your faithfulness!"			
Isaiah 6:3: "And one called to another and said: 'Holy, holy, holy is the LORD of hosts; the whole earth is full of his glory!'"			
Luke 2:14: "Glory to God in the highest, and on earth peace among those with whom he is pleased!"			
1 Corinthians 10:31: "So, whether you eat or drink, or whatever you do, do all to the glory of God."			

CREATION: Lesson 4, Scripture Exploration

Review the verse you started to explore last week.

"And one called to another and said: 'Holy, holy, holy is the LORD of hosts; the whole earth is full of his glory!'"

—Isaiah 6:3

1. Who is speaking in this verse? (Read Isaiah 6:1–2 for clues.)

2. Who is the speaker talking about? Circle the name in the verse.
3. What is the speaker doing in this verse? Why are they talking?

4. What is filled with God's glory? Circle the words.
5. Is just part of the earth filled with God's glory?
   Circle your answer.

   YES or NO

6. Can something be kind of filled with God's glory?
   Circle any clue words in the verse, then circle your answer.

   YES or NO

IMAGE: Lesson 1, Focus Activity

What can you see when you look at someone in the mirror? What details or actions can you see reflected in the mirror?

When you look in a mirror, can you see what the person is thinking? Why or why not?

Is the image in the mirror exactly the same as the person? Why or why not?

IMAGE: Lesson 1, Activity

Circle the word IMAGE in the verse.	*Who is this verse about?*	*In this verse, what do you hear about what it means to image?*
Colossians 1:15: "He is the image of the invisible God, the firstborn of all creation."		
Romans 8:29: "For those whom he foreknew he also predestined to be conformed to the image of his Son, in order that he might be the firstborn among many brothers."		
2 Corinthians 3:18: "And we all, with unveiled face, beholding the glory of the Lord, are being transformed into the same image from one degree of glory to another. For this comes from the Lord who is the Spirit."		
Colossians 3:10: ". . . and have put on the new self, which is being renewed in knowledge after the image of its creator."		

IMAGE: Lesson 1, Scripture Exploration

"So God created man in his own image, in the image of God he created him; male and female he created them."

—Genesis 1:27

1. Circle any words that refer to our Creator.
2. Circle any words that refer to creations that are made in the image of God.
3. Underline the word "image."
4. In your own words, what does this verse say to you?

IMAGE: Lesson 2, Focus Activity

People are made in God's image, but other creatures are not.

Draw examples of image bearers and non-image bearers in the correct boxes below.

These people are made in the image of God:

These other creatures are NOT made in the image of God:

IMAGE: Lesson 2, Activity

What are some things that only people can do that other creatures can't? Write and sketch one skill or ability in each box below.

IMAGE: Lesson 2, Scripture Exploration

Review the verse you started to explore last week.

"So God created man in his own image, in the image of God he created him; male and female he created them."

—Genesis 1:27

1. Circle any words that refer to our Creator.
2. Circle any words that refer to creations that are made in the image of God.
3. Underline the word "image."
4. How does this verse connect to you?

IMAGE: Lesson 3, Focus Activity

In the chart below, draw or list things that are alike (a little like each other), and things that are not alike (things that are different.)

ALIKE	NOT ALIKE

IMAGE: Lesson 3, Activity

Write the verse.	*What quality does the verse describe?*	*Describe a time when the Holy Spirit helped you display this quality.*	*Can you display this quality perfectly all the time? How does God the Trinity respond?*
Colossians 3:9–10			
Romans 5:8			
John 14:31			

IMAGE: Lesson 3, Scripture Exploration

"Whom have I in heaven but you? And there is nothing on earth that I desire besides you. My flesh and my heart may fail, but God is the strength of my heart and my portion forever."

—Psalm 73:25–26

1. Circle words that refer to the thing the author desires most.
2. Cross out words that refer to things that ultimately fail.
3. Put a box around words that describe the forever source of strength.
4. Could you honestly pray this verse? Describe a time when you desired something more than God.

5. How does Jesus respond?

IMAGE: Lesson 4, Focus Activity

What are some of your responsibilities at home? Responsibilities are things that you are in charge of doing, and that other people expect you to do. Your responsibilities might include chores, taking care of your room, and more.

List some of your responsibilities in words or pictures in the box below.

IMAGE: Lesson 4, Activity

Complete the Venn diagram below. What is true about only God? What is true about only people? What are some ways that people are a little like God?

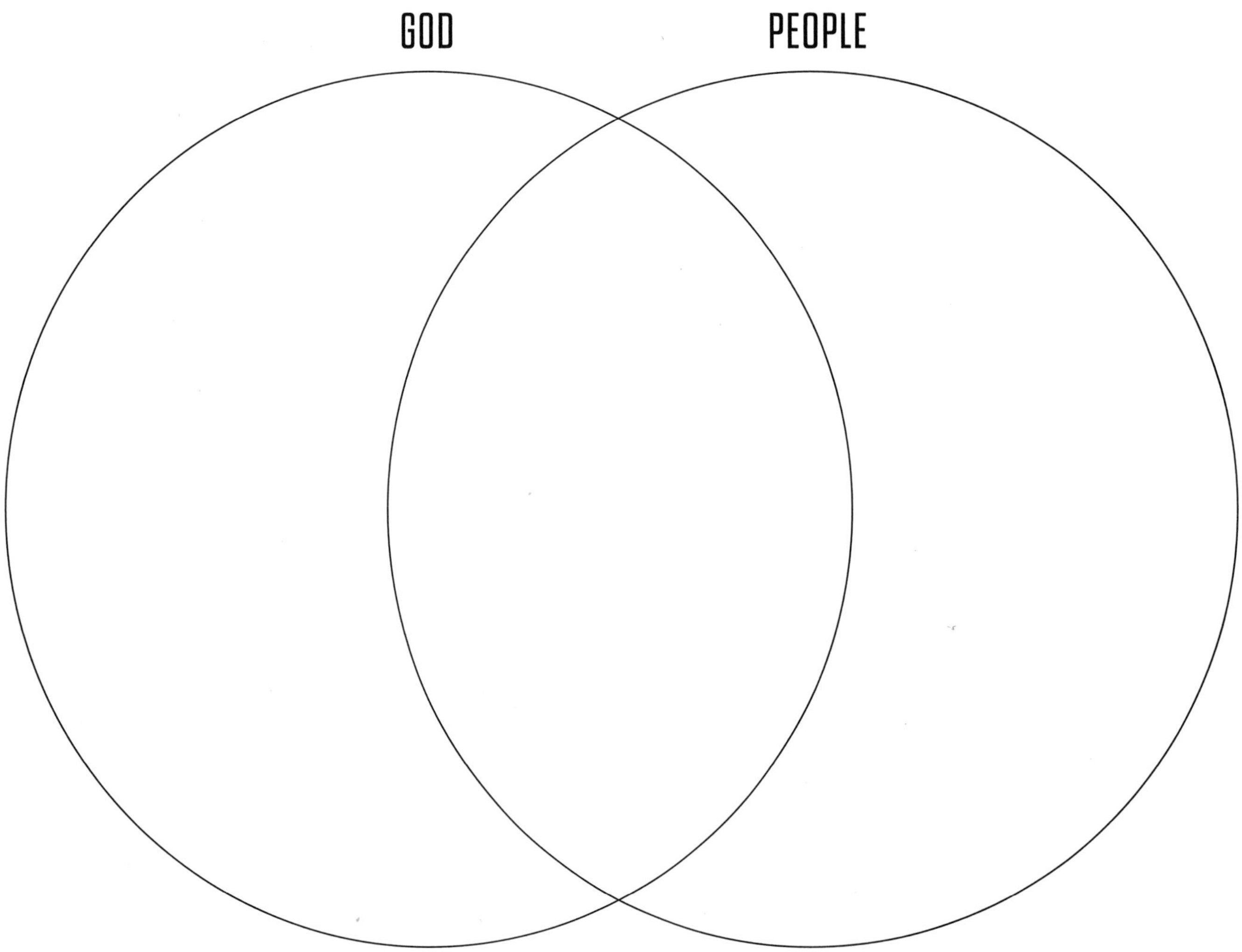

IMAGE: Lesson 4, Scripture Exploration

Review the verses you started to explore last week.

"Whom have I in heaven but you? And there is nothing on earth that I desire besides you. My flesh and my heart may fail, but God is the strength of my heart and my portion forever."

—Psalm 73:25–26

1. Circle words that refer to the thing the author desires most.
2. Cross out words that refer to things that ultimately fail.
3. Put a box around words that describe the forever source of strength.
4. How does this verse connect to your own life?

FALL: Lesson 1, Focus Activity

Are there problems in the world? Stop and sketch or write about at least two problems you have seen or heard of.

FALL: Lesson 1, Activity

Imagine that you are watching a movie of the fall, and the movie pauses at the moment when Adam and Eve realize what they have done. Draw a picture of what you see, and feel free to add words.

FALL: Lesson 1, Scripture Exploration

"Therefore, just as sin came into the world through one man, and death through sin, and so death spread to all men because all sinned."

—Romans 5:12

1. Circle any words that refer to sin.
2. Put a box around any words that describe the result of sin.
3. Underline any words that describe who sins.
4. Who is "one man" describing?

....

5. How does this verse describe you?

....

....

....

....

....

....

FALL: Lesson 2, Focus Activity

Take a moment to remember what you learned last week about when Adam and Eve disobeyed God. Who was there? What happened? Sketch a picture of what happened in the box below.

FALL: Lesson 2, Activity

In the verse below, circle the word SIN.	*What does this verse tell you about WHO sins?*	*What does this verse tell you about when a person begins to sin?*
Psalm 51:5: "Behold, I was brought forth in iniquity, and in sin did my mother conceive me."		
Romans 5:14: "Yet death reigned from Adam to Moses, even over those whose sinning was not like the transgression of Adam, who was a type of the one who was to come."		
Romans 5:17: "For if, because of one man's trespass, death reigned through that one man, much more will those who receive the abundance of grace and the free gift of righteousness reign in life through the one man Jesus Christ."		

FALL: Lesson 2, Scripture Exploration

Review the verse you started to explore last week.

"Therefore, just as sin came into the world through one man, and death through sin, and so death spread to all men because all sinned."

—Romans 5:12

1. Circle any words that refer to sin.
2. Put a box around any words that describe the result of sin.
3. Underline any words that describe who sins.
4. Who is "one man" describing?

....

5. Who sins? How does this verse connect to you and to other people you know?

....

....

....

....

....

....

FALL: Lesson 3, Focus Activity

Summarize what you already know about the fall using the five Ws.

WHO was involved?

WHAT happened?

WHERE did it happen?

WHEN did it happen?

WHY did it happen?

FALL: Lesson 3, Activity

Who sins? Write a one-sentence summary describing who sins.

Do your parents sin?	YES	or	NO
Do your friends sin?	YES	or	NO
Do your neighbors sin?	YES	or	NO
Do your enemies sin?	YES	or	NO
Do your teachers sin?	YES	or	NO
Do you sin?	YES	or	NO

How is God calling you to respond to sin with the story of Jesus the Rescuer?

Do your parents need Jesus?	YES	or	NO
Do your friends need Jesus?	YES	or	NO
Do your neighbors need Jesus?	YES	or	NO
Do you need Jesus?	YES	or	NO

FALL: Lesson 3, Scripture Exploration

"For as in Adam all die, so also in Christ shall all be made alive."

—1 Corinthians 15:22

1. Circle the word that describes who sins.
2. Put a box around the word that describes the result of sin.
3. Put a star above the name of the Rescuer who conquered sin and death.
4. Underline the word that describes our condition when God changes our hearts to love Jesus. (Hint: we are no longer dead in our sins.)
5. Jesus' work on the cross was powerful enough to rescue the whole world. Put a triangle above the word that describes who Jesus' work was powerful enough to save.
6. In your own words, what is this verse saying?

FALL: Lesson 4, Focus Activity

Who sins? Stop and think about people you know who sin. (Hint: *everyone sins*, including you!) In the box below, sketch yourself and at least one other person who sins.

FALL: Lesson 4, Activity

Connect the fall to God's Big Story by describing the five Ws of the Rescue that God promised would come. Feel free to use your Bible or to discuss in your Community Group while you work.

WHO would God send?

WHAT would he do?

WHERE would he do it?

WHEN would he do it?

WHY would he do it?

FALL: Lesson 4, Scripture Exploration

Review the verse you started to explore last week.

"For as in Adam all die, so also in Christ shall all be made alive."
—1 Corinthians 15:22

1. Circle the word that describes who sins.
2. Put a box around the word that describes the result of sin.
3. Put a star above the name of the Rescuer who conquered sin and death.
4. Underline the word that describes our condition when God changes our hearts to love Jesus. (Hint: we are no longer dead in our sins.)
5. Jesus' work on the cross was powerful enough to rescue the whole world. Put a triangle above the word that describes who Jesus' work was powerful enough to save.

7. How does this verse connect to your own life?

COVENANT: Lesson 1, Focus Activity

Think of a time you made a promise, or someone made a promise to you.

WHO made the promise?

Sketch the person here:

WHO was the promise to?

Sketch the person here:

WHAT was the promise?

Was the promise kept? YES or NO

Do people always keep their promises? YES or NO

COVENANT: Lesson 1, Activity

Circle the word NOAH in the verse.	*What does this verse tell you about who God is?*	*What does this verse tell you about who you are?*
Isaiah 54:9–10: "'This is like the days of Noah to me: as I swore that the waters of Noah should no more go over the earth, so I have sworn that I will not be angry with you, and will not rebuke you. For the mountains may depart and the hills be removed, but my steadfast love shall not depart from you, and my covenant of peace shall not be removed,' says the LORD, who has compassion on you."		
Matthew 24:36–39: "But concerning that day and hour no one knows, not even the angels of heaven, nor the Son, but the Father only. For as were the days of Noah, so will be the coming of the Son of Man. For as in those days before the flood they were eating and drinking, marrying and giving in marriage, until the day when Noah entered the ark, and they were unaware until the flood came and swept them all away, so will be the coming of the Son of Man."		
Hebrews 11:7: "By faith Noah, being warned by God concerning events as yet unseen, in reverent fear constructed an ark for the saving of his household. By this he condemned the world and became an heir of the righteousness that comes by faith."		

COVENANT: Lesson 1, Scripture Exploration

"Behold, I establish my covenant with you and your offspring after you."

—Genesis 9:9

1. Circle the word that refers to the person talking in this verse.
2. Who is talking? ……………………………………
3. Put a box around the word that means "promise."
4. Underline the word that refers to Noah.
5. Put a star above any words that refer to YOU.
6. In your own words, what is this verse saying?

……………………………………………………………………

……………………………………………………………………

……………………………………………………………………

……………………………………………………………………

……………………………………………………………………

……………………………………………………………………

COVENANT: Lesson 2, Focus Activity

Think of a time you broke a promise, or someone broke a promise they made to you.

WHO made the promise?

Sketch the person here:

WHO was the promise to?

Sketch the person here:

WHAT was the promise?

Do people always keep their promises? YES or NO

COVENANT: Lesson 2, Activity

Sketch the reminder that God created in the sky to tell us about his Forever Promise:

Then write what shape the rainbow reminds you of. Why might it be pointing up?

COVENANT: Lesson 2, Scripture Exploration

Review the verse you started to explore last week.

"Behold, I establish my covenant with you and your offspring after you."

—Genesis 9:9

1. Circle the word that refers to the person talking in this verse.
2. Who is talking? ____________________
3. Put a box around the word that means "promise."
4. Underline the word that refers to Noah.
5. Put a star above any words that refer to YOU.
6. How does this verse connect to your own life?

____

____

____

____

7. What promise is God making to you?

____

____

____

____

COVENANT: Lesson 3, Focus Activity

Write as many three-word phrases as you can describing what you know about covenants.

Example: *God's* *unbreaking* *promises*

Draw a speed sketch of one of God's promises you know about in the box below.

COVENANT: Lesson 3, Activity

Circle the word PROMISE in the verses.	*What do these verses teach you about who God is?*	*What do these verses teach you about who you are?*
Romans 4:13: "For the promise to Abraham and his offspring that he would be heir of the world did not come through the law but through the righteousness of faith."		
Romans 4:16–18: "That is why it depends on faith, in order that the promise may rest on grace and be guaranteed to all his offspring—not only to the adherent of the law but also to the one who shares the faith of Abraham, who is the father of us all, as it is written, 'I have made you the father of many nations'—in the presence of the God in whom he believed, who gives life to the dead and calls into existence the things that do not exist. In hope he believed against hope, that he should become the father of many nations, as he had been told, 'So shall your offspring be.'"		
Romans 4:20–21: "No unbelief made him waver concerning the promise of God, but he grew strong in his faith as he gave glory to God, fully convinced that God was able to do what he had promised."		

COVENANT: Lesson 3, Scripture Exploration

"And I will establish my covenant between me and you and your offspring after you throughout their generations for an everlasting covenant, to be God to you and to your offspring after you."

—Genesis 17:7

1. Circle any words that refer to the speaker.
2. Who is speaking in this verse? ....
3. Put a box around the word that means "promise."
4. Underline any words that refer to YOU.
5. Put a star above the word that describes how long the covenant lasts.
6. Will God's Forever Promise ever end? YES or NO

7. Put a triangle above any words describing what God promises.
8. In your own words, what is this verse saying?

....

....

....

....

....

....

COVENANT: Lesson 4, Focus Activity

Think of a time when you had to wait for something. You were expecting something, but it didn't happen right away.

Draw what happened in the box below.

COVENANT: Lesson 4, Activity

Answer the following questions to describe what you know about God's covenant with Abraham and how it connects to your life.

WHO did God make a promise to?

WHAT did God promise?

WHY might God have made this promise? *(Hint: connect it to God's Big Story!)*

Did Abraham obey God?

Did God keep his promise to Abraham?

Will God keep his promises to you? Why do you think so?

COVENANT: Lesson 4, Scripture Exploration

Review the verse you started to explore last week.

"And I will establish my covenant between me and you and your offspring after you throughout their generations for an everlasting covenant, to be God to you and to your offspring after you."

—Genesis 17:7

1. Circle any words that refer to the speaker.
2. Who is speaking in this verse? ....
3. Put a box around the word that means "promise."
4. Underline any words that refer to YOU.
5. Put a star above the word that describes how long the covenant lasts.
6. Will God's Forever Promise ever end? YES or NO
7. Put a triangle above any words describing what God promises.
8. How does this verse connect to your own life?

....

....

....

....

....

....

INCARNATION: Lesson 1, Focus Activity

Superheroes capture our imagination with their superhuman abilities. Wolverine can rapidly heal from injury. Invisible Woman can become invisible at will. Nitro can reform his own body after it explodes. Superman can fly. The Hulk has superhuman power. Aquaman can breathe underwater. Spiderman can climb walls. Wonder Woman can understand any language. Infinity is all-knowing. The Silver Surfer can manipulate gravity. Doomsday can resurrect form death. Kitty Pryde can pass through solid matter. And the Flash has superhuman speed.

Many children, and more than a few adults, have wondered what it would be like for a human being to have superhuman abilities. Yet Christian theology has something even more amazing because, unlike the superheroes, our Superhero truly lived, and his powers exceed those of comic book lore.

—Pastor Mark Driscoll (*Doctrine*, 209)

Jesus is the Hero of God's Big Story. He is more powerful, more heroic, and more loving than any hero before or since. However, lots of times in the world today we hear about superheroes. Right away we know a big difference between superheroes and Jesus: superheroes are fake, but Jesus is real. Complete the following Venn diagram to think about the similarities and differences between Jesus and superheroes. Consider the following questions while you work:

- What are some of the powers that Jesus has as God? How did he show them when he lived on the earth as both God and man?
- Who is the strongest hero of all?

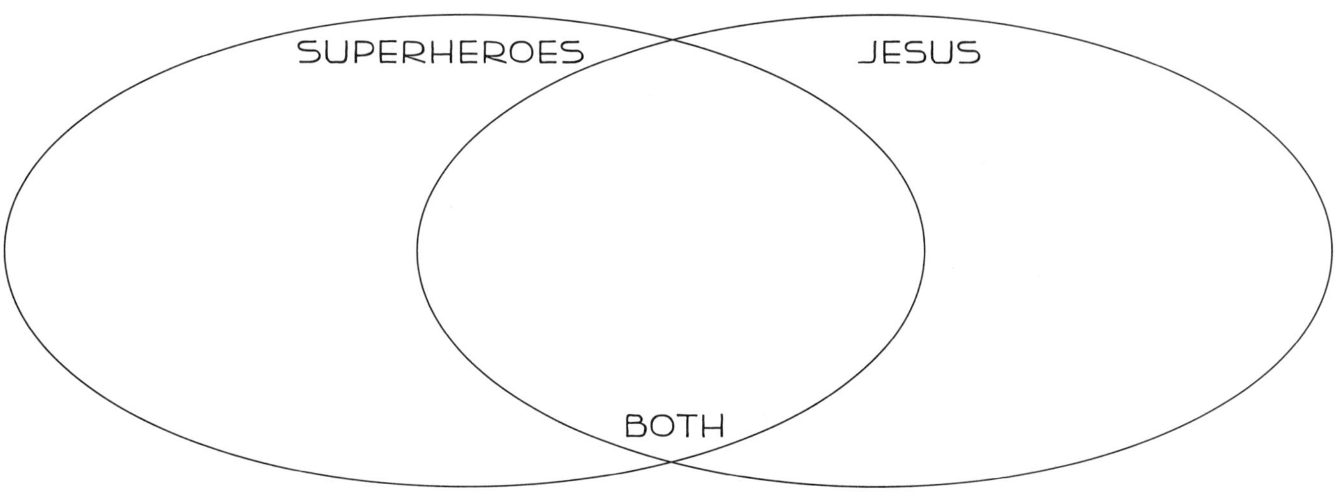

INCARNATION: Lesson 1, Activity

Complete this graphic organizer to explore who declares that Jesus is God throughout Scripture. Notice that Jesus is declared to be God in both the Old Testament and the New Testament by both people who love and follow Jesus, and people who do not.

Scripture	*Who is speaking?*	*Does the speaker love Jesus? Why do you think so?*	*Does the speaker declare that Jesus is God? Write the proof here.*
John 1:1: "In the beginning was the Word, and the Word was with God, and the Word was God."			
Isaiah 9:6: "For to us a child is born, to us a son is given; and the government shall be upon his shoulder, and his name shall be called Wonderful Counselor, Mighty God, Everlasting Father, Prince of Peace."			
Philippians 2:5–7: "Have this mind among yourselves, which is yours in Christ Jesus, who, though he was in the form of God, did not count equality with God a thing to be grasped, but emptied himself, by taking the form of a servant, being born in the likeness of men."			
Mark 1:24: "'What have you to do with us, Jesus of Nazareth? Have you come to destroy us? I know who you are—the Holy One of God.'"			

INCARNATION: Lesson 1, Scripture Exploration

"And the Word became flesh and dwelt among us, and we have seen his glory, glory as of the only Son from the Father, full of grace and truth."

—John 1:14

1. Circle the words that refer to Jesus.
2. Underline the words that describe what Jesus is like.
3. Put a box around the words that describe where Jesus lived in the middle of God's Big Story.
4. In your own words, what is this verse saying?

INCARNATION: Lesson 2, Focus Activity

Jesus the Son was born on the earth as a baby, just like every other person on the earth.

In the box below, sketch a picture of Jesus as a baby.

INCARNATION: Lesson 2, Activity

List three-word phrases describing some of the things that Jesus did or experienced as a man. (Hint: Think of things that every human needs or feels.)

Example:	*He*	*slept*	*often*
	He	*got*	*hungry*

INCARNATION: Lesson 2, Scripture Exploration

Review the verse you started to explore last week.

"And the Word became flesh and dwelt among us, and we have seen his glory, glory as of the only Son from the Father, full of grace and truth."

—John 1:14

1. Circle the words that refer to Jesus.
2. Underline the words that describe what Jesus is like.
3. Put a box around the words that describe where Jesus lived in the middle of God's Big Story.
4. How does this verse connect to you? Specifically, how does the phrase "we have seen his glory" connect to you?

INCARNATION: Lesson 3, Focus Activity

Brainstorm examples of people and things that are powerful. Complete each sentence, and then sketch what you wrote below the words. Then stop and think: who is the most powerful of all?

The most powerful machine is ______________________.	The most powerful sports star is ______________________.
The most powerful smell is ______________________.	The most powerful taste is ______________________.
The most powerful idea is ______________________.	The most powerful sight is ______________________.

But who is perfectly and totally powerful?

INCARNATION: Lesson 3, Activity

Scripture	***In your own words, what is happening in this verse?***	***What does this teach you about what God is like? God is _________.***
Mark 1:14–15: "Now after John was arrested, Jesus came into Galilee, proclaiming the gospel of God, and saying, 'The time is fulfilled, and the kingdom of God is at hand; repent and believe in the gospel.'"		
Mark 1:27–28: "And they were all amazed, so that they questioned among themselves, saying, 'What is this? A new teaching with authority! He commands even the unclean spirits, and they obey him.' And at once his fame spread everywhere throughout all the surrounding region of Galilee."		
Mark 1:40–42: "And a leper came to him, imploring him, and kneeling said to him, 'If you will, you can make me clean.' Moved with pity, he stretched out his hand and touched him and said to him, 'I will; be clean.' And immediately the leprosy left him, and he was made clean."		
Choose another New Testament verse that tells you about who Jesus is. Write the verse here.		

INCARNATION: Lesson 3, Scripture Exploration

"For we do not have a high priest who is unable to sympathize with our weaknesses, but one who in every respect has been tempted as we are, yet without sin."

—Hebrews 4:15

1. Circle the words that refer to Jesus.
2. Can Jesus sympathize with our weaknesses? *Circle one:*

   YES or NO

3. Was Jesus tempted like you are? *Circle one:*

   YES or NO

4. Put a box around the words that describe whether Jesus sinned in response to the temptation that he faced.

5. In your own words, what is this verse saying?

INCARNATION: Lesson 4, Focus Activity

Have you ever done something loving? Have you seen someone else do something loving? In the box below, draw at least one example of someone doing something loving.

Who did the most loving thing anyone has ever done?
What did he do? Why?

INCARNATION: Lesson 4, Activity

In your Community Group, brainstorm as many examples as you can of things Jesus did during his life on this earth that show that he is God, and that he is perfectly and totally powerful. Write one sentence to describe each example.

For more ideas, look at a children's Bible like *The Jesus Storybook Bible* or *The Gospel Story Bible*.

- ....
- ....
- ....
- ....
- ....
- ....
- ....
- ....
- ....
- ....
- ....
- ....
- ....
- ....
- ....

INCARNATION: Lesson 4, Scripture Exploration

Review the verse you started to explore last week.

"For we do not have a high priest who is unable to sympathize with our weaknesses, but one who in every respect has been tempted as we are, yet without sin."

—Hebrews 4:15

1. Circle the words that refer to Jesus.
2. Can Jesus sympathize with our weaknesses? *Circle one:*
   YES or NO
3. Was Jesus tempted like you are? *Circle one:*
   YES or NO
4. Put a box around the words that describe whether Jesus sinned in response to the temptation that he faced.
5. How does this verse connect to you?

INRI

CROSS: Lesson 1, Focus Activity

In the boxes provided, sketch what you know about Jesus' part in living out God's Rescue Plan as both God and man. Jesus knew about the plan from before the beginning, and agreed to live it out. Feel free to add words to describe your sketches.

JESUS COMES:

JESUS DIES:

JESUS LIVES:

CROSS: Lesson 1, Activity

Scripture	*In your own words, what is happening in this verse?*	*What does this verse teach you about God's Rescue Plan?*
Luke 22:44: "And being in an agony he prayed more earnestly; and his sweat became like great drops of blood falling down to the ground."		
Luke 22:49–51: "And when those who were around him saw what would follow, they said, 'Lord, shall we strike with the sword?' And one of them struck the servant of the high priest and cut off his right ear. But Jesus said, 'No more of this!' And he touched his ear and healed him."		
Luke 22:63–65: "Now the men who were holding Jesus in custody were mocking him as they beat him. They also blindfolded him and kept asking him, 'Prophesy! Who is it that struck you?' And they said many other things against him, blaspheming him."		
Luke 22:66–70: "When day came, the assembly of the elders of the people gathered together, both chief priests and scribes. And they led him away to their council, and they said, 'If you are the Christ, tell us.' But he said to them, 'If I tell you, you will not believe, and if I ask you, you will not answer. But from now on the Son of Man shall be seated at the right hand of the power of God.' So they all said, 'Are you the Son of God, then?' And he said to them, 'You say that I am.'"		

CROSS: Lesson 1, Scripture Exploration

"For our sake he made him to be sin who knew no sin, so that in him we might become the righteousness of God."

—2 Corinthians 5:21

1. Who became sin? ....

2. Did Jesus ever sin? *Circle one:*

   YES or NO

3. Circle the part of the verse that tells whether Jesus ever sinned.

4. Put a box around the word(s) that describe what we become in God's eyes because of Jesus.

5. In your own words, what is this verse saying?

INRI

CROSS: Lesson 2, Focus Activity

Think of a time you or someone you know got hurt. In the box below, tell what happened using words or pictures.

CROSS: Lesson 2, Activity

How did Jesus suffer? Brainstorm some of the ways he was hurt. Then, use the five Ws to describe the scene of the crucifixion.

WHO was there?

WHAT happened?

WHERE did it happen?

WHEN did it happen?

WHY did it happen?

CROSS: Lesson 2, Scripture Exploration

Review the verse you started to explore last week.

"For our sake he made him to be sin who knew no sin, so that in him we might become the righteousness of God."

—2 Corinthians 5:21

1. Who became sin? ....

2. Did Jesus ever sin? *Circle one:*

   YES or NO

3. Circle the part of the verse that tells whether Jesus ever sinned.

4. Put a box around the word(s) that describe what we become in God's eyes because of Jesus.

5. How does this verse connect to you?

....

....

....

....

....

....

INRI

CROSS: Lesson 3, Focus Activity

Sketch a picture showing what you know about the cross. Who was there? What was happening? Where did it happen? Include as many details as you can in your picture.

CROSS: Lesson 3, Activity

Scripture	*In your own words, what is going on in this verse?*	*What does this verse teach you about who Jesus is?*
Romans 5:10–11: "For if while we were enemies we were reconciled to God by the death of his Son, much more, now that we are reconciled, shall we be saved by his life. More than that, we also rejoice in God through our Lord Jesus Christ, through whom we have now received reconciliation."		
Luke 23:33: "And when they came to the place that is called The Skull, there they crucified him, and the criminals, one on his right and one on his left."		
Luke 23:34: "And Jesus said, 'Father, forgive them, for they know not what they do.' And they cast lots to divide his garments."		
Luke 23:42–43: "And he said, 'Jesus, remember me when you come into your kingdom.' And he said to him, 'Truly, I say to you, today you will be with me in Paradise.'"		
Choose another New Testament verse about the cross. Write the verse here.		

CROSS: Lesson 3, Scripture Exploration

"And being found in human form, he humbled himself by becoming obedient to the point of death, even death on a cross."

—Philippians 2:8

1. Who was found in human form? ____________
2. Underline the words that describe how Jesus humbled himself.
3. Put a box around the words that describe how Jesus died.
4. In your own words, what is this verse saying?

____

____

____

____

____

____

INRI

CROSS: Lesson 4, Focus Activity

Think of a time when you have paid for something.
What did you pay for? How did you pay for it?
Draw or describe your experience in the box below.

Jesus also paid for something.
What did he pay for? How did he pay?

CROSS: Lesson 4, Activity

How does it make you feel to think about how Jesus died? How does it make you feel to know *why* he died?

Write a two-sentence summary explaining your thoughts in response to each question.

When I think about how Jesus died, I feel . . .

When I think about why Jesus died, I feel . . .

CROSS: Lesson 4, Scripture Exploration

Review the verse you started to explore last week.

"And being found in human form, he humbled himself by becoming obedient to the point of death, even death on a cross."

—Philippians 2:8

1. Who was found in human form? ____________
2. Underline the words that describe how Jesus humbled himself.
3. Put a box around the words that describe how Jesus died.
4. How does this verse connect to you?

____

____

____

____

____

____

RESURRECTION: Lesson 1, Focus Activity

Write a three-sentence summary of what you know about the cross. (If you need ideas, check your workbook pages from last week.) Then, draw a quick sketch illustrating what you wrote.

THREE-SENTENCE SUMMARY:

SKETCH:

RESURRECTION: Lesson 1, Activity

Scripture	*What is going on in this verse?*	*How does this verse show that Jesus is really alive again?*
Luke 24:13–15: "That very day two of them were going to a village named Emmaus, about seven miles from Jerusalem, and they were talking with each other about all these things that had happened. While they were talking and discussing together, Jesus himself drew near and went with them."		
Luke 24:29–30: "But they urged him strongly, saying, 'Stay with us, for it is toward evening and the day is now far spent.' So he went in to stay with them. When he was at table with them, he took the bread and blessed and broke it and gave it to them."		
Luke 24:38–40: "And he said to them, 'Why are you troubled, and why do doubts arise in your hearts? See my hands and my feet, that it is I myself. Touch me, and see. For a spirit does not have flesh and bones as you see that I have.' And when he had said this, he showed them his hands and his feet."		

RESURRECTION: Lesson 1, Scripture Exploration

"Jesus said to her, 'I am the resurrection and the life. Whoever believes in me, though he die, yet shall he live, and everyone who lives and believes in me shall never die. Do you believe this?'"

—John 11:25–26

1. Underline the word that states who is talking.
2. Circle the words that Jesus uses to describe himself.
3. Who is Jesus talking to? People who ______________________ .
4. Put a box around the words that describe what happens to people who believe after they die.
5. In your own words, what are these verses saying?

RESURRECTION: Lesson 2, Focus Activity

Think of a time you were surprised by something. You expected one thing to happen, but something different happened instead. In the box below, tell what happened using words or pictures.

How do you think Jesus' friends felt when they saw that he was alive again?

RESURRECTION: Lesson 2, Activity

Was Jesus really alive again? How do you know? List as many examples as you can of things Jesus did on the earth in his better-than-before body.

- ....
- ....
- ....
- ....
- ....
- ....
- ....
- ....
- ....
- ....
- ....
- ....
- ....
- ....

RESURRECTION: Lesson 2, Scripture Exploration

Review the verses you started to explore last week.

"Jesus said to her, 'I am the resurrection and the life. Whoever believes in me, though he die, yet shall he live, and everyone who lives and believes in me shall never die. Do you believe this?'"

—John 11:25–26

1. Underline the word that states who is talking.
2. Circle the words that Jesus uses to describe himself.
3. Who is Jesus talking to? People who ______________ .
4. Put a box around the words that describe what happens to people who believe after they die.
5. The last sentence of verse 26 is a question. Answer the question on the lines below.

____

____

____

____

RESURRECTION: Lesson 3, Focus Activity

Think of a time when something changed you: maybe you liked something for the first time, or thought of something in a different way. Use the five Ws to describe the experience.

WHO was there?

WHERE were you?

WHEN did it happen?

WHAT happened?

WHY did it change you? How were you different?

RESURRECTION: Lesson 3, Activity

Read the following Scripture verses from both before and after the resurrection. As you read, watch to see how Peter changed when he received the Holy Spirit and saw that Jesus is alive.

Scripture	*Is this verse before or after the resurrection?*	*Is Peter worshiping Jesus here? Is he telling others about Jesus?*
Luke 22:54–57: "Then they seized him and led him away, bringing him into the high priest's house, and Peter was following at a distance. And when they had kindled a fire in the middle of the courtyard and sat down together, Peter sat down among them. Then a servant girl, seeing him as he sat in the light and looking closely at him, said, 'This man also was with him.' But he denied it, saying, 'Woman, I do not know him.'"		
Luke 22:58: "And a little later someone else saw him and said, 'You also are one of them.' But Peter said, 'Man, I am not.'"		
Luke 22:59–60: "And after an interval of about an hour still another insisted, saying, 'Certainly this man also was with him, for he too is a Galilean.' But Peter said, 'Man, I do not know what you are talking about.' And immediately, while he was still speaking, the rooster crowed."		
Acts 2:37–41: "Now when they heard this they were cut to the heart, and said to Peter and the rest of the apostles, 'Brothers, what shall we do?' And Peter said to them, 'Repent and be baptized every one of you in the name of Jesus Christ for the forgiveness of your sins, and you will receive the gift of the Holy Spirit. For the promise is for you and for your children and for all who are far off, everyone whom the Lord our God calls to himself.' And with many other words he bore witness and continued to exhort them, saying, 'Save yourselves from this crooked generation.' So those who received his word were baptized, and there were added that day about three thousand souls."		

RESURRECTION: Lesson 3, Scripture Exploration

"And he who was seated on the throne said, 'Behold, I am making all things new.' Also he said, 'Write this down, for these words are trustworthy and true.'"

—Revelation 21:5

1. Underline the words that refer to who is talking in this verse.
2. The person talking in this verse is ______________ .
3. Is Jesus making just some things new? *Circle one:*
   SOME THINGS or ALL THINGS
4. Does "all things" include you? *Circle one:*
   YES or NO
5. Circle the words that Jesus uses to describe his words.

6. In your own words, what is this verse saying?

____

____

____

____

____

____

RESURRECTION: Lesson 4, Focus Activity

Think of a time something or someone you know changed: they started out one way, then became another way. After they changed, they were not the same.

In the boxes below, draw what they were like before and after.

BEFORE:

AFTER:

RESURRECTION: Lesson 4, Activity

If you believe in Jesus, what will happen to you after you die? Will you have a body again someday? Write as many three-word phrases as you can to describe what will happen.

Example:	*Better*	*than*	*before*

RESURRECTION: Lesson 4, Scripture Exploration

Review the verse you started to explore last week.

"And he who was seated on the throne said, 'Behold, I am making all things new.' Also he said, 'Write this down, for these words are trustworthy and true.'"

—Revelation 21:5

1. Underline the words that refer to who is talking in this verse.
2. The person talking in this verse is ______________.
3. Is Jesus making just some things new? *Circle one:*
   SOME THINGS or ALL THINGS
4. Does "all things" include you? *Circle one:*
   YES or NO
5. Circle the words that Jesus uses to describe his words.
6. How does this verse connect to you?

____

____

____

____

____

____

CHURCH: Lesson 1, Focus Activity

Get your mind going about the word "church" by completing the following sentences. Don't worry about whether there is a right answer—just write what you think! Then, sketch what you think of when you hear the word "church."

The church is ______________________________.

The church has ______________________________.

The church does lots of things, including ______________________________.

The purpose of the church is to ______________________________.

Sketch what you think of when you hear the word "church."

CHURCH: Lesson 1, Activity

Scripture	*What does this passage teach you about the church?*
Acts 2:44–45: "And all who believed were together and had all things in common. And they were selling their possessions and belongings and distributing the proceeds to all, as any had need."	
Acts 2:46–47: "And day by day, attending the temple together and breaking bread in their homes, they received their food with glad and generous hearts, praising God and having favor with all the people. And the Lord added to their number day by day those who were being saved."	
Acts 4:31: "And when they had prayed, the place in which they were gathered together was shaken, and they were all filled with the Holy Spirit and continued to speak the word of God with boldness."	
Acts 4:32–33: "Now the full number of those who believed were of one heart and soul, and no one said that any of the things that belonged to him was his own, but they had everything in common. And with great power the apostles were giving their testimony to the resurrection of the Lord Jesus, and great grace was upon them all."	

CHURCH: Lesson 1, Scripture Exploration

"Christ loved the church and gave himself up for her."

—Ephesians 5:25b

1. Circle the word that refers to Jesus.
2. Underline action words of things that Jesus did.
3. Who did Jesus give himself up for? ....
4. Did Jesus give himself up for a building? *Circle one:*

YES or NO

5. In your own words, what is this verse saying?

....

....

....

....

CHURCH: Lesson 2, Focus Activity

The church is all people who believe in Jesus as the Savior from sin. Who do you know that is part of the church? Are you part of the church?

In the box below, draw at least one person you know who is part of the church.

CHURCH: Lesson 2, Activity

Complete the sentences below again considering what you've learned about the church. Sketch a picture of what you think of now when you hear the word "church."

The church is ______________________________.

The church has ______________________________.

The church does lots of things, including ______________________________.

The purpose of the church is to ______________________________.

Sketch what you think of when you hear the word "church."

CHURCH: Lesson 2, Scripture Exploration

Review the verse you started to explore last week.

"Christ loved the church and gave himself up for her."

—Ephesians 5:25b

1. Circle the word that refers to Jesus.
2. Underline action words of things that Jesus did.
3. Who did Jesus give himself up for? ....
4. Did Jesus give himself up for a building? *Circle one:*

YES or NO

5. How does this verse connect to you?

....

....

....

....

CHURCH: Lesson 3, Focus Activity

It's time to get your brain going on the word "mission." A mission is a special purpose or job that someone has. Complete each sentence below to identify what the person's mission is, then sketch an example of them completing their mission.

A teacher's mission is to ______________________________ .	Spiderman's mission is to ______________________________ .
A baseball player's mission is to ______________________________ .	____________'s mission is to ______________________________ .

Jesus has a special mission for his people. We'll find out more about it today . . .

CHURCH: Lesson 3, Activity

Scripture	*Who is talking in this verse?*	*What does this verse teach you about the special mission of God's people?*
Matthew 28:19–20: "'Go therefore and make disciples of all nations, baptizing them in the name of the Father and of the Son and of the Holy Spirit, teaching them to observe all that I have commanded you. And behold, I am with you always, to the end of the age.'"		
Acts 1:8: "'But you will receive power when the Holy Spirit has come upon you, and you will be my witnesses in Jerusalem and in all Judea and Samaria, and to the end of the earth.'"		
John 20:21: "Jesus said to them again, 'Peace be with you. As the Father has sent me, even so I am sending you.'"		
Can you find another verse describing the special mission? Write it here.		

CHURCH: Lesson 3, Scripture Exploration

"'Go therefore and make disciples of all nations, baptizing them in the name of the Father and of the Son and of the Holy Spirit, teaching them to observe all that I have commanded you. And behold, I am with you always, to the end of the age.'"

—Matthew 28:19–20

1. Jesus is commanding his people to make ____________________.
2. In your own words, a "disciple" is someone who ____________________

____.
3. Circle the words that describe things Jesus tells us to do with his disciples.
4. Jesus is with people who believe in him (*circle one*):

SOMETIMES or ALWAYS

CHURCH: Lesson 4, Focus Activity

What is the special mission that Jesus gave the church? Tell about the mission in the space below using words or pictures.

CHURCH: Lesson 4, Activity

What are some of the things God's people did in the New Testament to carry out Jesus' special mission? List as many examples as you can think of below.

- ....
- ....
- ....
- ....
- ....

CHURCH: Lesson 4, Scripture Exploration

Review the verses you started to explore last week.

"'Go therefore and make disciples of all nations, baptizing them in the name of the Father and of the Son and of the Holy Spirit, teaching them to observe all that I have commanded you. And behold, I am with you always, to the end of the age.'"

—Matthew 28:19–20

1. Jesus is commanding his people to make ______________________.
2. In your own words, a "disciple" is someone who ______________________

   ____.
3. Circle the words that describe things Jesus tells us to do with his disciples.
4. These verses are often called the "Great Commission." Do you see the word "mission" inside the word "commission"? Circle it! A commission is when someone gives a special mission. In your own words, what is the Great Commission?

____

____

____

____

____

____

WORSHIP: Lesson 1, Focus Activity

Think of the word "worship." What do you picture when you think of the word? Sketch it in the space below.

Now, brainstorm a list of things that people worship.

- ....
- ....
- ....
- ....
- ....

WORSHIP: Lesson 1, Activity

In the Bible, God gives us many examples of times when his people were worshiping him. He also gives examples of times his people worshiped someone or something other than him. Examine the following passages from Scripture to determine what people were worshiping, and how the gospel of Jesus applies.

Scripture	*Who or what were people worshiping?*	*How does the gospel of Jesus apply here?*
Romans 1:25: ". . . because they exchanged the truth about God for a lie and worshiped and served the creature rather than the Creator, who is blessed forever! Amen."		
Exodus 32:7–8: "And the LORD said to Moses, 'Go down, for your people, whom you brought up out of the land of Egypt, have corrupted themselves. They have turned aside quickly out of the way that I commanded them. They have made for themselves a golden calf and have worshiped it and sacrificed to it and said, 'These are your gods, O Israel, who brought you up out of the land of Egypt!'"		
Genesis 3:13: "Then the LORD God said to the woman, 'What is this that you have done?' The woman said, 'The serpent deceived me, and I ate.'"		
Acts 24:14: "But this I confess to you, that according to the Way, which they call a sect, I worship the God of our fathers, believing everything laid down by the Law and written in the Prophets."		

WORSHIP: Lesson 1, Scripture Exploration

"'But the hour is coming, and is now here, when the true worshipers will worship the Father in spirit and truth, for the Father is seeking such people to worship him.'"

—John 4:23

1. Underline the words that name people who love and follow Jesus.
2. Circle the word that means to love and live for someone or something.
3. Put a box around the person we are created to worship.
4. Does God the Father want us to worship him? *Circle one:*

YES or NO

5. In your own words, what is this verse saying?

....

....

....

....

WORSHIP: Lesson 2, Focus Activity

Who worships? Do you worship? Do other people you know worship? (Hint: every person worships all the time!)

In the box below, draw at least three people you know who worship.

WORSHIP: Lesson 2, Activity

Brainstorm and sketch examples of things that God's people sometimes do together at the church building to worship Jesus.

On each line, write what people do. Then sketch an example in the box.

WORSHIP: Lesson 2, Scripture Exploration

Review the verse you started to explore last week.

"'But the hour is coming, and is now here, when the true worshipers will worship the Father in spirit and truth, for the Father is seeking such people to worship him.'"

—John 4:23

1. Underline the words that name people who love and follow Jesus.
2. Circle the word that means to love and live for someone or something.
3. Put a box around the person we are created to worship.
4. Does God the Father want us to worship him? *Circle one:*

YES or NO

5. How does this verse connect to you?

....

....

....

....

WORSHIP: Lesson 3, Focus Activity

Many things change. They start out one way, then become another way. Something about them is new or different. In each box, brainstorm ways that each thing can change.

How can the weather change?	How can what someone likes to do for fun change?
How can someone's dreams change?	How can a heart change?

WORSHIP: Lesson 3, Activity

What are some of the pieces of a person's life that change when you believe in Jesus? In each box, brainstorm and write or draw how each piece might be different in response to who Jesus is.

A heart might change by:	Thoughts might change by:
Words might change by:	Actions might change by:

WORSHIP: Lesson 3, Scripture Exploration

"Therefore, if anyone is in Christ, he is a new creation. The old has passed away; behold, the new has come."

—2 Corinthians 5:17

1. Underline the words "in Christ." What do you think it means to be "in Christ?"

2. Circle the words that describe the fact that when you believe in Jesus, you have a new heart.
3. Put a box around the words "the old has passed away." What do you think this means?

4. In your own words, what is this verse saying?

WORSHIP: Lesson 4, Focus Activity

Every person worships all of the time. This means that you are worshiping someone or something in the morning, in the afternoon, and in the evening—all of the time!

In the boxes below, sketch the times of day when you are worshiping.

In the morning . . .

In the afternoon . . .

In the evening . . .

WORSHIP: Lesson 4, Activity

Scripture	*What is going on in this verse?*	*What is Saul like? What is he doing? What does he want? What does he really, really love and live for?*
Acts 9:1–2: "But Saul, still breathing threats and murder against the disciples of the Lord, went to the high priest and asked him for letters to the synagogues at Damascus, so that if he found any belonging to the Way, men or women, he might bring them bound to Jerusalem."		
Acts 9:3–9: "Now as he went on his way, he approached Damascus, and suddenly a light from heaven shone around him. And falling to the ground he heard a voice saying to him, 'Saul, Saul, why are you persecuting me?' And he said, 'Who are you, Lord?' And he said, 'I am Jesus, whom you are persecuting. But rise and enter the city, and you will be told what you are to do.' The men who were traveling with him stood speechless, hearing the voice but seeing no one. Saul rose from the ground, and although his eyes were opened, he saw nothing. So they led him by the hand and brought him into Damascus. And for three days he was without sight, and neither ate nor drank."		
Acts 9:17b–19: "And laying his hands on him he said, 'Brother Saul, the Lord Jesus who appeared to you on the road by which you came has sent me so that you may regain your sight and be filled with the Holy Spirit.' And immediately something like scales fell from his eyes, and he regained his sight. Then he rose and was baptized; and taking food, he was strengthened. For some days he was with the disciples at Damascus."		

WORSHIP: Lesson 4, Scripture Exploration

Review the verse you started to explore last week.

"Therefore, if anyone is in Christ, he is a new creation. The old has passed away; behold, the new has come."

—2 Corinthians 5:17

1. Underline the words "in Christ." What do you think it means to be "in Christ?"

2. Circle the words that describe the fact that when you believe in Jesus, you have a new heart.
3. Put a box around the words "the old has passed away." What do you think this means?

4. How does this verse connect to you?

STEWARDSHIP: Lesson 1, Focus Activity

Brainstorm and sketch some of your favorite things in the boxes below.

My favorite toy:	A friend I love: ....
My favorite thing to wear:	My favorite treat: ....

Who is really the owner of these things?

STEWARDSHIP: Lesson 1, Activity

Read 2 Chronicles 2–4, then answer the questions based on the verses below to unpack an example of stewardship in the Old Testament.

Scripture	*What is going on in this verse?*	*Do you think Solomon is stewarding God's gifts? Why do you think so?*
2 Chronicles 2:1: "Now Solomon purposed to build a temple for the name of the LORD, and a royal palace for himself."		
2 Chronicles 2:4: "'Behold, I am about to build a house for the name of the LORD my God and dedicate it to him for the burning of incense of sweet spices before him, and for the regular arrangement of the showbread, and for burnt offerings morning and evening, on the Sabbaths and the new moons and the appointed feasts of the LORD our God, as ordained forever for Israel.'"		
2 Chronicles 2:5: "'The house that I am to build will be great, for our God is greater than all gods.'"		
Can you find another verse that describes Solomon as a good steward? Write it here.		

STEWARDSHIP: Lesson 1, Scripture Exploration

"As each has received a gift, use it to serve one another, as good stewards of God's varied grace."

—1 Peter 4:10

1. Underline the word that describes what God has given to each.
2. Put a box around the words that describe what we are supposed to do with the gift.
3. Circle the word that means "to take care of something."
4. Write an example of God's gifts: ....

5. In your own words, what is this verse saying?

....

....

....

....

STEWARDSHIP: Lesson 2, Focus Activity

Think of a time you saw someone take extra special care of something. They were stewarding it by taking care of it well.

Sketch your memory in the box below.

STEWARDSHIP: Lesson 2, Activity

What are some of the things God has given you to take care of? Sketch and describe one example in each box below.

STEWARDSHIP: Lesson 2, Scripture Exploration

Review the verse you started to explore last week.

"As each has received a gift, use it to serve one another, as good stewards of God's varied grace."

—1 Peter 4:10

1. Underline the word that describes what God has given to each.
2. Put a box around the words that describe what we are supposed to do with the gift.
3. Circle the word that means "to take care of something."
4. Write an example of God's gifts: ....

5. How does this verse connect to you?

....

....

....

....

STEWARDSHIP: Lesson 3, Focus Activity

What are some of your favorite things that you like to do with your time? Draw at least three examples in the box below.

STEWARDSHIP: Lesson 3, Activity

Read 2 Corinthians 9:6–15, then answer the questions below.

Scripture	*In your own words, what is this verse saying?*	*What does this verse teach you about what it means to be a good steward?*
2 Corinthians 9:7: "Each one must give as he has decided in his heart, not reluctantly or under compulsion, for God loves a cheerful giver."		
2 Corinthians 9:8: "And God is able to make all grace abound to you, so that having all sufficiency in all things at all times, you may abound in every good work."		
2 Corinthians 9:11: "You will be enriched in every way to be generous in every way, which through us will produce thanksgiving to God."		
2 Corinthians 9:12: "For the ministry of this service is not only supplying the needs of the saints but is also overflowing in many thanksgivings to God."		
2 Corinthians 9:15: "Thanks be to God for his inexpressible gift!"		

STEWARDSHIP: Lesson 3, Scripture Exploration

"As it is written, 'He has distributed freely, he has given to the poor; his righteousness endures forever.'"

—2 Corinthians 9:9

1. Who do you think "he" is? ....
2. Underline the words that describe what Jesus has done.
3. Circle the word that describes how he has done it.
4. Put a box around the words that describe who he gives to.
5. Does Jesus' goodness ever end? *Circle one*:

   YES or NO

6. In your own words, what is this verse saying?

STEWARDSHIP: Lesson 4, Focus Activity

What is something that you are good at?

Sketch or describe your talent in the box below.

STEWARDSHIP: Lesson 4, Activity

What are you really good at? How could you steward your talent well? In each box below, describe or sketch an example of a way you can steward your talents.

MY TALENT: ______

I can steward my talent by . . .

MY TALENT: ______

I can steward my talent by . . .

STEWARDSHIP: Lesson 4, Scripture Exploration

Review the verse you started to explore last week.

"As it is written, 'He has distributed freely, he has given to the poor; his righteousness endures forever.'"

—2 Corinthians 9:9

1. Who do you think "he" is? ______________________
2. Underline the words that describe what Jesus has done.
3. Circle the word that describes how he has done it.
4. Put a box around the words that describe who he gives to.
5. Does Jesus' goodness ever end? *Circle one*:

YES or NO

6. How does this verse connect to you?

____

____

____

____

____

____

KINGDOM: Lesson 1, Focus Activity

Using the prompts below, write down everything you know about kings. In each box, jot down whatever comes to mind. Feel free to add illustrations if you'd like.

What a king looks like:

What a king is in charge of:

How a king acts:

Who a king loves:

Do you know who the King of kings is? Today we'll find out . . .

KINGDOM: Lesson 1, Activity

Scripture	*In your own words, what is this verse saying?*	*What does this verse teach you about Jesus' kingdom?*
Revelation 1:5: ". . . and from Jesus Christ the faithful witness, the firstborn of the dead, and the ruler of kings on earth. To him who loves us and has freed us from our sins by his blood."		
Revelation 21:4: "'He will wipe away every tear from their eyes, and death shall be no more, neither shall there be mourning, nor crying, nor pain anymore, for the former things have passed away.'"		
Revelation 22:3–4: "No longer will there be anything accursed, but the throne of God and of the Lamb will be in it, and his servants will worship him. They will see his face, and his name will be on their foreheads."		
Choose another verse from Revelation that teaches you about Jesus' kingdom. Write the verse here.		

KINGDOM: Lesson 1, Scripture Exploration

"'Your kingdom come, your will be done, on earth as it is in heaven.'"

—Matthew 6:10

1. Who do you think "your" is referring to? ______
2. Who is the King of the kingdom? ______
3. Underline the words that describe whose will rules in the new creation.
4. Circle the word that describes where you are now.
5. Put a box around the word that describes what will come down to earth some day, when Jesus makes all things new.

6. In your own words, what is this verse saying?

______

______

______

______

KINGDOM: Lesson 2, Focus Activity

Imagine that you wake up tomorrow and the city where you live has no sin and no problems. What would your city be like?

Draw what you think it would be like in the box below.

KINGDOM: Lesson 2, Activity

What will the new earth be like? Will it be a good Forever Home? Sketch a picture of what you think the new earth will look like in the box below.

KINGDOM: Lesson 2, Scripture Exploration

Review the verse you started to explore last week.

"'Your kingdom come, your will be done, on earth as it is in heaven.'"

—Matthew 6:10

1. Who do you think "your" is referring to? ....
2. Who is the King of the kingdom? ....
3. Underline the words that describe whose will rules in the new creation.
4. Circle the word that describes where you are now.
5. Put a box around the word that describes what will come down to earth some day, when Jesus makes all things new.

6. How does this verse connect to you?

....

....

....

....

KINGDOM: Lesson 3, Focus Activity

What do you know about Jesus' Forever Kingdom? If you need ideas, check your workbook pages from last week. Then, using the lines provided, write as many three-word phrases as you can describing Jesus' kingdom.

Example:	*No*	*more*	*death*

KINGDOM: Lesson 3, Activity

Scripture	***Does this verse describe something that is already or not yet?***	***What does this verse teach you about Jesus' kingdom?***
Mark 1:14–15: "Now after John was arrested, Jesus came into Galilee, proclaiming the gospel of God, and saying, 'The time is fulfilled, and the kingdom of God is at hand; repent and believe in the gospel.'"		
John 4:23–24: "'But the hour is coming, and is now here, when the true worshipers will worship the Father in spirit and truth, for the Father is seeking such people to worship him. God is spirit, and those who worship him must worship in spirit and truth.'"		
Revelation 22:20: "He who testifies to these things says, 'Surely I am coming soon.' Amen. Come, Lord Jesus!"		
Choose another verse from the New Testament that tells about how Jesus' kingdom is already and not yet. Write the verse here.		

KINGDOM: Lesson 3, Scripture Exploration

"'He will wipe away every tear from their eyes, and death shall be no more, neither shall there be mourning, nor crying, nor pain anymore, for the former things have passed away.'"

—Revelation 21:4

1. Who do you think "he" is? ....
2. Will there be death in the better-than-before world?
   Circle one:
   YES or NO
3. Underline the words that describe what Jesus will do in his not-yet kingdom.
4. Will there be sadness in the better-than-before world?
   Circle one:
   YES or NO

5. In your own words, what is this verse saying?

....

....

....

....

....

....

KINGDOM: Lesson 4, Focus Activity

Jesus' kingdom has already begun in the hearts of people who believe in him as the Savior from sin.

In the box below, sketch at least one person you know who is part of Jesus' Forever Kingdom.

KINGDOM: Lesson 4, Activity

Compare and contrast the already and not yet of Jesus' kingdom. Complete the Venn diagram below to describe the ways in which Jesus' kingdom is "already" and the ways in which it is "not yet."

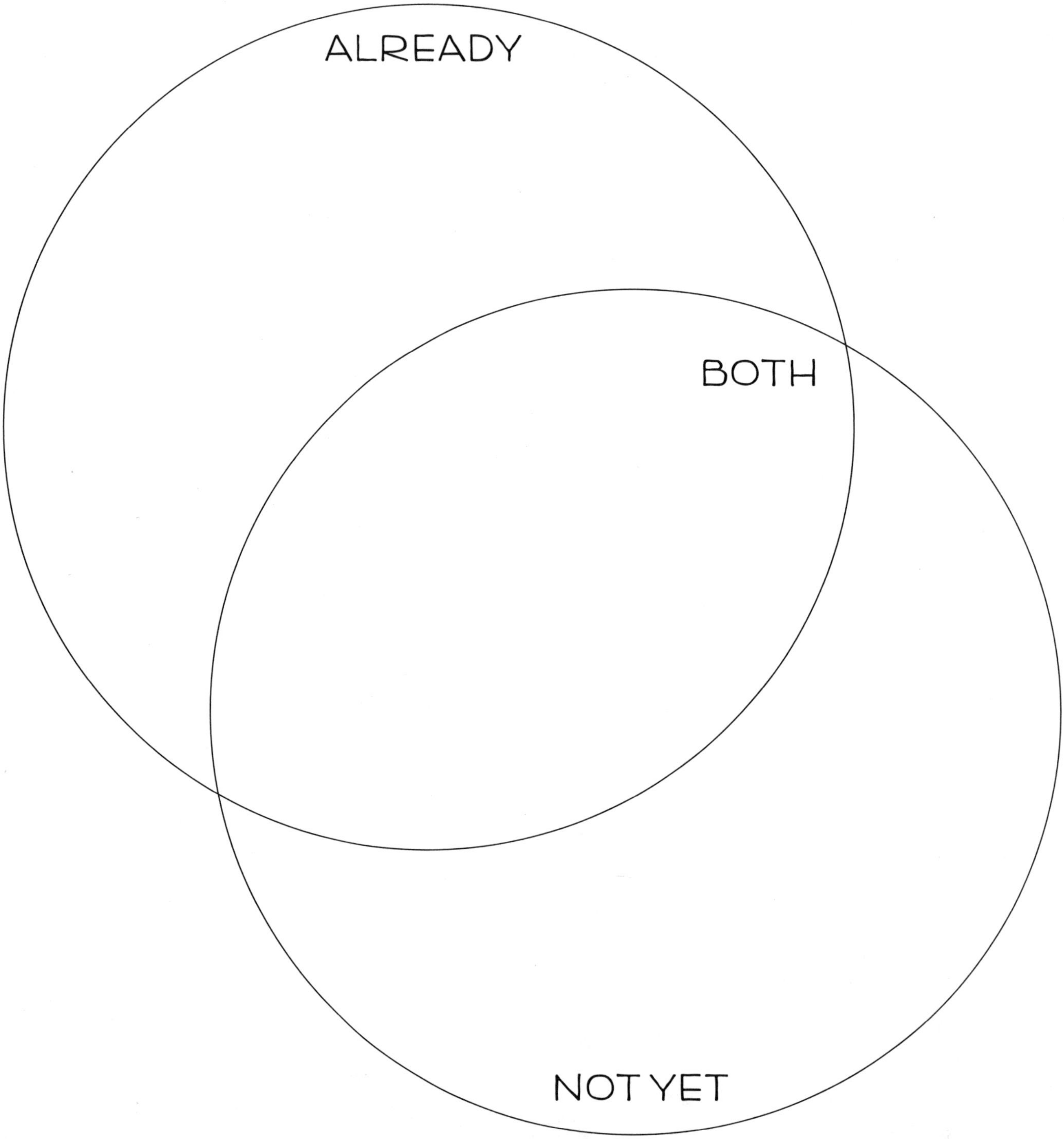

KINGDOM: Lesson 4, Scripture Exploration

Review the verse you started to explore last week.

"'He will wipe away every tear from their eyes, and death shall be no more, neither shall there be mourning, nor crying, nor pain anymore, for the former things have passed away.'"

—Revelation 21:4

1. Who do you think "he" is? ....
2. Will there be death in the better-than-before world? *Circle one*:

   YES or NO
3. Underline the words that describe what Jesus will do in his not-yet kingdom.
4. Will there be sadness in the better-than-before world? *Circle one*:

   YES or NO

5. How does this verse connect to you?

....

....

....

....

....

....